How is wine made?

Translated by Angela Caldwell

Éditions Jean-Paul Gisserot
www.editions-gisserot.eu

Introduction

Wine has been part of our culture since ancient times. Most of us appreciate it for its taste but we usually know little about how it is made.

There are various stages involved in turning bunches of grapes into glasses of wine and they are complex. They require the skills of an expert and wine production today is a science. To be successful, vignerons have to take account of many different factors that draw on knowledge of physics, chemistry and biology. Enlightened advice from a qualified oenologist has also become essential.

Before he begins actually making the wine, however, a vigneron has a whole year's work ahead of him among the vines.

At the end of autumn, the posts and wires or nylon lines that support the vines are carefully checked and replaced if necessary. Pruning, a vital early stage in the production process,

n Alsace. Photo by Renault.

takes up much of the winter and any shoots pruned are removed or crushed.

In the spring, when the sap rises and the buds and leaves begin to appear, further pruning takes place to remove surplus shoots. Only the branches that guarantee good-quality grapes are retained. A good vigneron always has an eye to the excellence of his wine and he may sometimes carry out "green harvesting", decreasing the density of bunches by causing some of them to fall off the plant before they ripen. He then removes the leaves from the vines to make it easier for the grapes to ripen and harvesters to pick them. In the meantime, he will also have treated the plants to fight diseases such as mildew and avoid the risk of rotting. Hoeing removes any weeds.

With the arrival of the grape harvest, he begins working in the wine cellar.

The next stage in the work will be particularly important. He will be creating the wine and, throughout the long, delicate production process, helping it to develop the essential qualities already in the grapes.

The grape harvest

Harvesting is one of the high points in a vigneron's calendar. It is a testament to the efforts he has made throughout the year to ensure the quality of his vines.

The work carried out in the vat room depends on the quality and quantity of the harvest.

At the same time, despite the fatigue, aches and pains that it sometimes causes, the harvest remains a festive, friendly experience for the grape pickers.

TIMING

In France, the grapes are picked between the months of August and November. The exact time varies depending on the years and the regions but the grapes must be fully ripe, usually containing high levels of sugar and low acidity.

THE FIRST SIGNS

To ensure that the time is right for harvesting, a grape grower will usually pick a few bunches of each variety. He weighs the individual grapes, presses them and has the juice tested. The oenologist can then work out the most appropriate time for the harvest.

There are, though, other criteria to consider before setting the date:

CRITERIA

Rainy days are best avoided. Fine weather is required for grape harvests.

Grapes affected by botrytis.
CIVB/V. Bengold.

The harvest usually begins with green grape varieties; they ripen earlier than black grapes.

Everybody knows that the harvest should be carried out as late as possible to produce a perfectly ripened grape that will give good wine. There are two types of maturity for black grapes – technological maturity (corresponding to the highest accumulation of sugars) and phenolic maturity, which occurs later and allows the winemaker to extract a maximum amount of tannins and colour from the skins. In green grapes, the right level of ripening will maintain the right balance between acidity and the freshness of the aroma. For sparkling wines, the grapes are picked before they reach technological maturity to preserve the acidity that best suits the wine's effervescence.

Manual picking in the Bordeaux area.
CIVB/Ph. Roy.

THE WINEMAKER'S DILEMMA

A winemaker has to bear all these criteria in mind while paying constant attention to the health of the crop because better may not always be best. By waiting too long for the ideal level of maturity, a wine crop can fall victim to its worst enemy – botrytis. If the infection is too severe, it damages the organoleptic qualities of the future wine and seriously impairs its colour. Indirectly, it can also cause various bacterial or yeast imbalances referred to as wine diseases. A healthy harvest is preferable by far, making the winemaker's job easier from every point of view. Hence the importance of careful picking and sorting of the grapes.

Grape picker's basket in the Bordeaux area. CIVB/Ph. Roy.

TWO TYPES OF HARVESTING

These days, there are two ways of harvesting grapes – manually or by machine.

MANUAL HARVESTING

Despite the spread of mechanisation, grapes are still harvested manually in many places using age-old methods, especially for high-quality red wines, sweet dessert wines and sparkling wines.

The pickers cut the grapes using secateurs and put them in a basket placed on the ground in front of them. When the baskets are full, they are collected in one of several ways:

Sometimes "porters" come and give the pickers empty baskets then carry away the full ones and pour the contents into holding bins on the back of the tractor or simply pour them into a trailer designed for this purpose.

Sometimes the porters carry a basket on their backs and pass along the rows at regular intervals. The pickers pour the contents of their buckets into the porters' baskets and the grapes are then poured into the trailer.

Another method also used at the present time by harvesters is to place the grapes in openwork crates. Once full, the crates are piled up on a support on the porters' backs. They are then taken to the trailer.

Manual picking is particularly useful because it allows for selection at the time of harvesting and an initial sorting of the grapes. When cutting bunches of grapes, experienced pickers remove any fruit that is mouldy, too dry or unripe and take any leaves or unwanted debris out of their baskets. If a trailer is not used, there is another advantage to this

Porter's basket in the Bordeaux area.
CIVB/François Ducasse.

method. It avoids packing the grapes too tightly, which can release the juice too quickly and possibly cause oxidation.

MECHANISED HARVESTING

In many vineyards, mechanical harvesters replaced human pickers in the 1970s.

A grape harvester is a piece of self-propelled or tow-behind agricultural machinery. It carries out several operations such as mechanised picking, the removal of stalks and the discarding of plant waste (leaves, petals or pieces of stem).

The machine functions by means of vibration. As it passes along the rows, it shakes the trellises causing the grapes to fall off the lines supporting them. The grapes drop onto a conveyor belt from which a succession of buckets carries them to containers. They are then poured into the trailers.

Although a mechanical harvester cannot achieve the same results as a person in terms of quality, and although driving a machine like this requires a great deal of care and attention, it still has a number of advantages. It is a fast method (it takes

Mechanical harvester. Photo by Vincent Dubourg.

Mechanical harvester in the Bordeaux area. CIVB/Cronenberger.

about two hours to cover a hectare of vines), which means that the grapes can be harvested more quickly in fine weather. It can also work at night. In fact, for any vigneron who owns such a piece of equipment, it is flexible, making it easy to monitor the level of maturity of the grapes on various plots of land. This flexibility is lost, however, if the equipment is shared by several vignerons or hired from an external contractor. Moreover, in some very hilly regions such as Moselle or Burgundy, it is almost impossible to use.

Mechanised harvesting is usually followed by sorting on a conveyor belt.

SORTING THE GRAPES

To produce sweet or sparkling wines, the grapes have to be picked by hand and only bunches suffering from noble rot or "botrytis", a fungus that slowly damages the skin, are selected. This means that pickers have to pass along the rows more than once, each time selecting only "good rotted grapes" and leaving on the vine grapes that are not yet sufficiently ripe. They also discard grapes that have rotted or become vinegary (acid rot) as they would give wine an unpleasant taste.

LATE HARVESTING:

Late harvests take place several weeks after the others, when the grapes have been left to ripen as much as possible. Noble rot will have developed on the fruit and become concentrated. Late harvests are commonplace in Alsace, especially for Riesling, Pinot Gris, Gewurztraminer and Muscat.

Of course, the yield from this very selective form of harvesting is very small.

Another way of concentrating the sugars, and a method used in late harvests in Alsace and other regions, is to let the bunches of grapes dry out on the vine. This is a technique known as "raisining".

A FEW TIPS:

Avoid harvesting in the rain. The moisture dilutes the grape juice.

Grapes should not be warm when they are brought into the vat room, otherwise they may begin to ferment or, in the case of white wines, make

Grape harvesting.
Photo by Jacques Dubourg.

Vines beside La Sauve-Majeure Abbey (Gironde). Photo by Gisserot.

racking more difficult (cf. chapter on vinification). In the same way, the grapes should always be taken to the vat room as quickly as possible. They should be picked in fine weather, but not at the hottest times of day.

Harvesting is quicker and more efficient if the vines have been correctly prepared, with recent pruning and the removal of leaves from the stems that are fruiting.

TRADITIONS

Whether carried out mechanically or by hand, the end of harvesting is always an opportunity for celebrations. Anybody involved in picking or sorting the grapes is invited to a high-quality meal that include the vineyard's best wines, in contrast to the ones served during picking known as "wines on lees" (*vins de lie*).

PREPARATION

Before the harvest, all the equipment in the vat room is serviced and prepared.

The tank in particular is carefully inspected, rigorously cleaned and all tartar removed to avoid the presence of impurities that might impair the vinification process. Its seal is also checked. The pipes through which the grapes pass on their way to the vats are washed and disinfected.

The equipment (press, destemmer, crusher, pumps etc.) is checked to make sure it is in working order.

Tractor and trailer. Photo by Vincent Dubourg.

RED WINE

ARRIVAL OF THE GRAPES

The grapes are brought to the cellar by tractor then destemmed before being sorted one or more times. They may or may not be crushed before being placed in vats or firkins.

DESTEMMING

Destemming the grapes is usually the first thing done when they arrive at the vat room. The process removes the grapes from the stalks. It is not obligatory but it is often recommended for the production of high-quality wine. Destemming limits any green taste and improves the taste of the wine while increasing the finesse of the tannins. Some winegrowers retain a portion of the stems to make up for a lack of tannins (Pinot Noir in Burgundy or Alsace) but this is less and less common today.

The stalks are removed by a destemmer, usually consisting of a perforated metal cylinder. A set of blades rotates the grapes which are ejected through the holes while the stalks and stems remain inside. The fruit and juice are then pumped to the vats while the stems are discarded from the machine.

SORTING

Sorting is carried out before or after destemming to remove any remaining waste such as leaves, pieces of stem or grapes that are either rotten or not

The grapes arrive at the vat room.
Photo by Renault.

Destemming the grapes.
Photo by Jacques Dubourg.

ripe. Workers stand at a vibrating sorting table that separates the unwanted waste from the fruit and eliminates any oxidised juice. Purists may sort the fruit twice (before and after destemming).

There are also automated sorting machines consisting of tanks in which the grapes float. Selection is done by density – the grapes containing the least sugar float to the top.

CRUSHING

After sorting and destemming, the grapes are crushed. This gently breaks open the fruit and releases its juice. At this point, the grapes are ready to ferment in vats. In days gone by, the pickers stomped on the grapes in their bare feet to crush them but now a machine is used. It consists of two rubber rollers that turn in opposite directions. There is a small space between them to avoid tearing the grape skins. This process is not used for Beaujolais wines, because fermentation is carried out inside the whole grapes.

TRANSFERRING THE GRAPES

After destemming, sorting and crushing the fruit, the grape must is piped into the vats using a pump designed to limit contact with the grapes.

TEMPERATURE CONTROL

The must requires a certain temperature as soon as it enters the vats, and in the subsequent stages of production, if it is to ferment correctly. Temperatures are therefore increased or decreased inside the vats as required until the correct level is achieved. Temperature control is essential.

The temperature is adjusted using a thermostat that sends water at the required temperature through the belts round the outside of the vats or into submerged, watertight stainless steel reservoirs.

In other types of equipment, it is the must itself which is circulated rather than the temperature-controlled water.

The must can be cooled in a tower by passing through pipes cooled by a liquid. It can be heated in a gas heater in which the temperature can be raised by passing the must through a heated container.

Sorting the grapes in the Bordeaux area. CIVB/Ph. Roy.

Trailer and sorting table. Photo by Vincent Dubourg.

WHITE WINE

Unlike red wine, white wine is fermented in the liquid phase i.e. without the grape skins or pips. The first stage in the process is pressing.

PRESSING

Pressing uses pressure to extract the grape juice. The quality of the end product will depend mainly on the quality of the equipment and the se-

Stems and transferring the grapes. Photo by Jacques Dubourg.

lection of the correct setting.

There are several types of press:

Some of them are known as continuous presses because the grapes are poured into them without a break. They cannot be used for some of the AOC wines because of the poor results they generally achieve. On the other hand, pneumatic or vertical hydraulic presses are becoming increasingly commonplace in cellars because the grapes are pressed gradually and the machinery can be very finely adjusted.

Whatever the equipment, the juice becomes increasingly hard, bitter or even grassy as the pressure increases. Because of this the vintner has to taste the musts at they leave the press in order to create the appropriate blends. The juice can then be taken to a vat for vinification (racking and fermentation).

A pump. Photo by Jacques Dubourg.

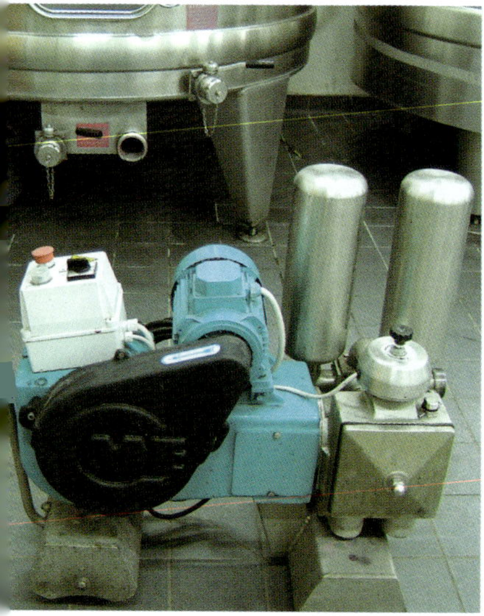

SULPHUR DIOXIDE

Over the past few years, it has been mandatory to include the words "Contains sulphur dioxide" on wine labels and this has raised many questions in consumers' minds. Yet the practice of adding SO2 is not only ancient; it is always recommended at certain key stages in winemaking, especially when the grapes reach the vat room. These days, though, dosing is done with increasing care and accuracy to limit the final quantities and avoid the side effects such as the "hangover" suffered by many drinkers in the evening or the next morning after drinking generous amounts of wine. Sulphur dioxide is added before fermentation and does not depend on the type of winemaking process used thereafter. The addition of sulphur dioxide (SO2) to the must, usually in liquid form, will slightly delay fermentation. In white wines, it will help to drag any matter in suspension down into the must. It will also avoid the spread of bacteria or parasitic yeasts and limit oxidation. The restorative product is used all the more commonly if the grapes har-

Temperature control.
Photo by Jacques Dubourg.

vested are of an inferior quality whereas vignerons who take proper care of their vines can, in certain years, significantly decrease the addition of SO2.

After destemming and crushing or pressing the grapes, there are still many more stages left in the wine-making process but they are not always the same. They vary depending on whether the wine being made is red, dry white, sweet white, dessert wine, rosé or sparkling.

A wine press. Photo by Jacques Dubourg.

Red wines

The winemaking process begins as soon as the grapes are placed in the stainless steel, fibreglass or concrete vats. Sometimes, the process is carried out in the age-old, traditional manner in firkins, gigantic barrels that are slightly truncated and laid on their sides. In this case, there is an exchange between the wood (oak) and the grapes over the first few years but this lessens over time as the firkin becomes increasingly inert.

At present, there is a move towards another, less traditional form of winemaking known as "integral vinification" in which the entire process is carried out directly in the barrels. Technically speaking, it has a number of drawbacks - the barrels have to be replaced frequently in order to achieve an elegant blend of tannins from the wood and the grapes.

Whatever the process used, however, the primary objectives of red wine production, possibly after cold maceration, are alcoholic fermentation followed by the extraction of tannins and hot maceration.

Skin contact maceration in the Bordeaux area. CIVB/Ph. Roy.

Drawing off in the Bordeaux area. CIVB/CVM.

PRIMARY OBJECTIVES

Cold maceration

At the beginning of the process, the pulp, pips and skins form a fairly smooth "soup" but the various ingredients gradually separate out under the effect of gravity. The juice released by crushing and the sheer weight of the fruit gradually builds up in the bottom of the vat while a more solid mass of skins and pips forms above it. This is called the "cap".

During this period of "pre-fermentation cold maceration", the juice takes on a colour and an aroma under the influence of the alcohol and by contact with the various ingredients. At this point, the maceration temperature has to be adjusted.

Drawing off with a candle in the Bordeaux area. CIVB/François Ducasse.

This is essential in order to avoid the proliferation of bacteria and parasitic yeasts that might compromise the wine. For maceration to be effective, the grapes must have been picked in the morning while they are still cold. If the fruit is too warm, it must be cooled using the heat exchangers in the columns or the cooling system in the vats.

The cold maceration stage is optional and can be adapted to produce certain types of wine or certain vintages. The decision on whether or not to use the process will be discussed by the vigneron and the oenologist.

At present, certain growers tend to prolong this stage, using modern techniques.

However long the process, the first fermentation must always begin within the first four or five days after placing the grapes in the vats.

Primary fermentation or alcoholic fermentation

Alcoholic fermentation is a natural process that is difficult to control but it is the keystone of the process that turns grape juice into wine. This is the stage that will show just what the grapes contain, including the hidden characteristics that are never revealed in fresh table grapes. Grape juice, for example, is becoming increasingly popular but it does not have the complexity of wine. Yet the complexity is not solely dependent on the alcohol. All fruit can ferment (particularly apples) but experience has shown that only grapes were capable of synthesising a host of aromatic molecules found in nature (in flowers, fruit, tree sap, plants etc.).

THE PRINCIPLES

Although fermentation involves a fairly complex chemical process, the principle behind it is very simple. It turns the fruit sugars into alcohol, mainly ethanol, thanks to the action of single-cell fungi called yeasts. The transformation is made easier by the chemical composition of the glucose or fructose molecules (our everyday "sugar") contained in the grapes, which is fairly similar to the chemical composition of ethanol.

THE PROCESS

The transformation takes place as a result of a set of chemical reactions that synthesise and reorganise the raw materials, producing not only the alcohol but all the other ingredients of wine as well (alcohols, esters, organic acids etc.).

How does this fermentation occur in the vat? The process is actually fairly anarchic. It occurs spontaneously when the temperature of the fruit reaches approximately 15°C and continues up to 25°C.

PUMPING OVER

During fermentation, the cellar worker carries out a series of operations known as "pumping over". This consists of drawing off the juice released by the crushing of the grapes, allowing it to breathe in a basin then re-injecting it into the top of the vat through a tourniquet that trickles the juice down onto the cap.

Pumping over can be carried out four times a day at the beginning of fermentation. Thereafter, the frequency and duration decrease and pumping over ceases altogether just before the end of the fermentation process called "AF" (alcoholic fermentation) by the technicians. Pumping over serves two purposes:

- it provides the yeasts with oxygen to speed up their metabolism and achieve fast fermentation,

- and it ensures maximum contact between the must and the marc to add agents to the future wine ("anthocyans" and "tannins" respectively) that will give it colour and body.

The frequency and duration of pumping over vary depending on the style of wine and the characteristics of the grape varieties. Generally speaking, the riper and more colourful the grape, the more frequent the mechanical process. In some regions, fermentation also includes extraction processes.

Extraction processes

Fermentation is a natural process but it is the vintner's experience that produces a wine with a deeper or lighter colour, more or less fruitiness and a higher or lower tannin content. Depending on local traditions and the types of wine being produced, various extraction methods are used and they are still being improved thanks to modern research:

RACK AND RETURN

In the Bordeaux area, vignerons use a process known as "*delestage*" or "rack and return". The liquid is drained from the vat halfway through the fermentation process. The must is then returned to the top of the vat, breaking up the cap and soaking it. The break-up of the marc produces a smoother blend of marc and juice and helps to extract the rich tannins

Wicking in the Bordeaux area. CIVB/Ph. Roy.

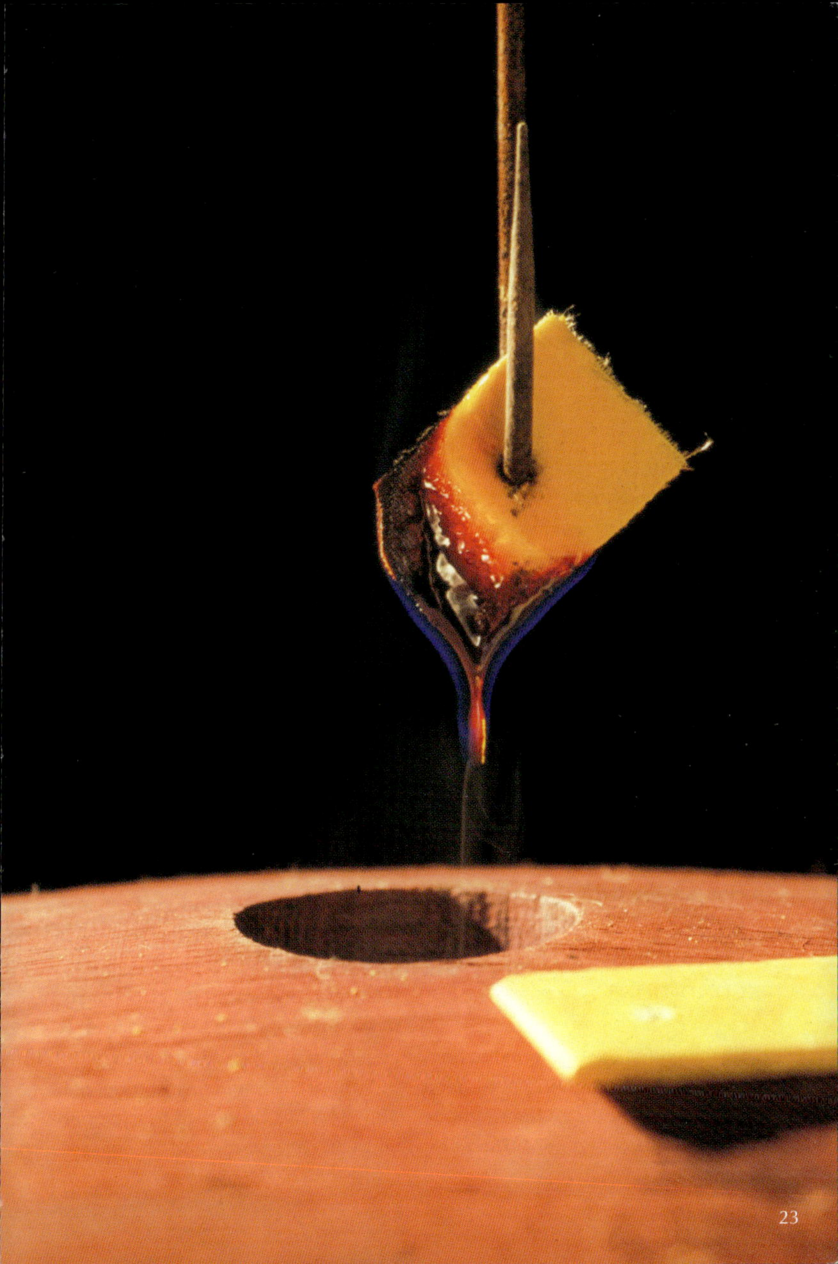

and colour from the grape skins. The process overcomes the adverse effects of pumping over, which tends to create channels within the marc, rather like an anthill, limiting the chemical exchanges.

PUNCH-DOWN

The other well-known method, used mainly in Burgundy, is punch-down. The vigneron forces pieces of marc down into the juice using a long wooden or metal pole with a square or circular tip. He repeats the operation across the entire surface of the must, breaking up the cap and increasing the area of exchange. It is a relatively labour-intensive technique that can only be done with high-quality grapes, otherwise it tends to develop plant-like aromas that are not popular today. Punch-downs require a great deal of care to avoid tearing the grape skins.

A bunch of Pinot Noir grapes.
Dubois/CIVC.

Hot maceration

PRELIMINARY CONDITIONS

By the end of the first fermentation, almost all the sugars have been turned into alcohol, giving the wine its final alcoholic content. The complex chemical reaction also releases a large quantity of energy, mainly in the form of heat. Depending on the heat-retaining capacity of the vats, more or less heat is removed and, in general, a vat that has a temperature of 18°C at the beginning of fermentation will have heated up to a temperature of 30°C by the end.

MACERATION

Usually the new wine is left to macerate with its marc while warm to add intensity to the colour and strengthen the various tannins. This process is particularly useful if a few grapes have been incorrectly crushed. It will always take longer for the juice trapped within them to degrade completely, forming alcohol.

The time taken for hot maceration varies depending on whether or not the winemaker can keep the vat at the right temperature (between 26 and 28°C). The length of time also depends on the results of daily tasting. Only by tasting the wine can the vintner judge the effects of the process on the wine's body. A few notes of bitterness and dryness indicate that the process has run its course.

During maceration, the surface of the cap is dampened with juice to avoid any acetic souring because the carbon dioxide released by fermentation gradually disappears and the wine is no longer protected. However, the maceration process should not be too long as this may alter the surface area of the must, or even the wine itself, allowing the cap to drop down to the bottom of the vat.

It is now time for the next stages in the process, in particular removal from the vat.

OTHER PROCESSES

Devatting and pressing

DEVATTING

Devatting takes place when the wine has acquired its usual appearance, with the exception of fairly heavy particles that give it a very cloudy aspect.

The lower taps on the vats are opened, releasing the "free run wine" by gravity or by means of a pump. This wine is then transferred into another vat or into barrels. The term "run wine" is used to describe light wines resulting from the draining of the vat without any mechanical action on the must. It usually describes the most elegant and most well-rounded wines.

PRESSING

After draining, the marc in the bottom of the vats can be transferred to the press. At this point, a worker usually has to climb into the vat and shovel the marc out into bins, or use a special pump to remove it. Since marc is very sensitive to oxidation, this process has to be done quickly. Pressing produces wines referred to as "press wines".

We will not go into the various types of wine press or pressing processes. Put simply, the quality of the end-product depends largely on the work of the winemaker and the science of winemaking. The quality of press wines, for example, can be altered if the marc is pressed too hard or too quickly and if the various pressing levels are wrongly calculated. In all, 15% of red wine production will depend on this process since this is the usual ratio of press wine to free run wine.

Second fermentation

The second fermentation is also known as malolactic fermentation because it breaks down the lactic acid contained in the wine, turning it into malic acid.

This stage has only been part of the winemaking process for half a century. Before that, it

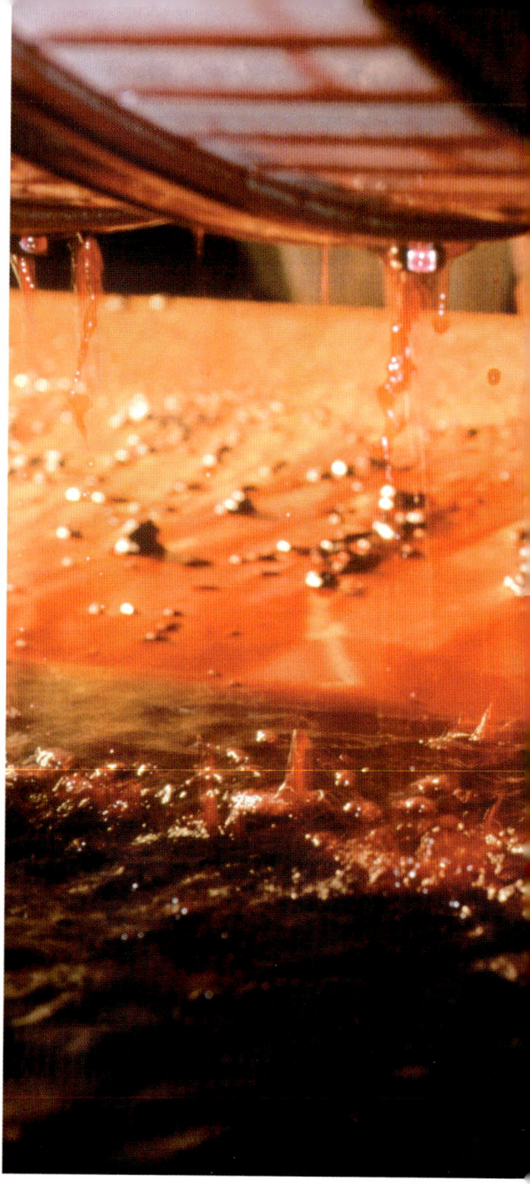

Pressing in the Bordeaux area. CIVB/Ph. Roy.

was not always used and, if it was, it was often done in springtime. Nowadays, this bacterial fermentation is done as soon as possible after devatting and pressing.

THE PROCESS

Second fermentation uses bacteria to break down the acids.

It is done when sulphur is added in the form of anhydrous sulphur or sulphur dioxide to protect the wine against a wide range of alterations. However, the level of active sulphur must be very low to allow the necessary bacteria to breed and work. Fast, clean malolactic fermentation enables the sulphur to protect the wine.

Winegrowers are always somewhat impatient during this stage of the process because the lactic acid produced by the bacteria is less tart than the impaired malic acid from the grapes.

ITS EFFECTS

Second fermentation lowers the wine's acidity, refines its aroma and makes it more pleasant to drink. Once this stage has been completed (at a temperature of approximately 22°C), red wines can begin their long, quiet, aging process, in tanks or barrels.

Aging

DEFINITION

Aging comprises all the stages between fermentation and bottling. In certain vineyards, the term is also used to describe the aging of bottles of wine in cellars.

THE VARIOUS STAGES

Aging can take place in a vat or in a barrel. If barrels are used, maintenance and hygiene are essential. Before placing the wine in barrels, sulphur wicks or pastilles are burnt in them to disinfect the wood and avoid any bacterial contamination.

The wine is usually racked several times, but at long intervals, to refine it gradually and separate it from the lees that sink to the bottom of vats or the concave side of barrels. Sometimes, though, a new technique is used, whereby the lees remain in contact with the red wine (winemakers do this with white wines in the Loire Valley). This is done to make the wine rounder and smoother, giving it a soft texture and a velvety mouthfeel.

Numerous other processes can be used. Some winemakers leave the wine alone. Others rack it according to lunar cycles or anticyclones. Still others filter it early while some never filter it at all.

Pinot Noir grapes.
CIVA/Colmar collection.

A new method specific to so-called "natural" wines has also developed. The winemaker uses no corrective processes, no fining, no filtering etc. Consumers have to judge for themselves whether or not the paucity of technical processes creates a more pleasurable experience on the palate.

AGING PERIODS

It takes time (at least a year) for young wines to become drinkable and of good quality. Oxygen then becomes a fearsome ally. It is needed to develop the wine but, at the same time, it is dangerous if present in excessive quantities because it destroys the aromas and makes the wine "chewy", "oxidised" or "stale".

"Nouveau" wines sold two or three months after the grapes are harvested are in a category of their own because they are produced using methods that emphasise the very powerful, but very simple, fermentation aromas. In some of these wines, the grapes are left whole during fermentation (carbonic maceration of Beaujolais nouveau wines). They are not crushed and the maceration period is very short. These wines have to be drunk when very young because their aromas are unstable and the low tannin content prevents them from aging well.

After aging comes the preparation of the bottles. We shall deal with this stage later because the process is the same for all wines, whatever the colour (red, rosé, clairet and white).

A glass of red in the Bordeaux area.
CIVB/Yann Lacombe.

White wines

Dry whites are made from green grapes, the only exceptions being champagne and sparkling wines, which can be made from black grapes such as Pinot Noir or Pinot Meunier.

PRELIMINARY PRECAUTIONS

A number of precautions have to be taken. The grapes must be harvested before they have fully ripened to preserve their floral and fruity aromas. The grapes must be in perfect condition to avoid any bitterness or unpleasant odours. Care must be taken when transporting the grapes to the vat room to avoid damage.

The winemaking processes are slightly different to those used for red wines but there are plenty of them. Making white wine requires a succession of pre-fermentation and alcoholic fermentation processes.

PRE-FERMENTATION PROCESSES

The period leading up to fermentation is particularly important. The quality of the wine depends on decisions taken at this point. Any pre-fermentation maceration is followed by extraction of the must and destemming.

CIVS document.

Vines in Riquewihr (Haut-Rhin). Photo by Renault.

PRE-FERMENTATION OR SKIN CONTACT MACERATION

This stage is not mandatory and is a recent development. It requires perfect fruit and extensive chilling facilities. The aim is to heighten the aroma of the wine and produce wines that explode in the nose. At the start of the process, the fruit is scraped and left to macerate for a few hours in a vat, in a press consisting of a sealed vat or, sometimes, in a holding bin if it is covered. CO2 is added in the form of ice or dry ice to cool the fruit and prevent oxidation or the development of microbes. The substances contained in the grape skins are naturally released, producing their specific aromas.

This process takes between 24 and 48 hours and the temperature must be carefully controlled to prevent the development of parasitic yeasts. It is commonly used in the Bordeaux area as well as other regions, particularly for Chardonnay, Gros Manseng and Muscat grapes. It is not recommended if the grapes are of poor quality because it amplifies any defects in the aromas (greenness, fungal smell etc.). This means that, in most cases, the process is used only by winemakers who can sort the grapes by means of manual picking or sorting on the vine before the grapes are picked by a mechanical harvester.

PRESSING

The juice has to be extracted quickly and carefully to avoid oxidation.

The vigneron has a number of options. He can place the grapes directly into the press or scrape them first then crush them to reduce their volume and pack more grapes into the press. This second method is risky because tearing the skins may damage the taste but, in some cases, it is preferable to leaving increasing numbers of trailers outside in front of the cellar in the heat. Last but not least, the grapes are pressed, preferably in a horizontal pneumatic press but other types of press can be equally successful if used carefully and controlled by hand. The aim is to separate the juice from the solids (skins, pips and, possibly, stalks) so that fermentation is carried out in a liquid phase.

The last juice pressed, which is of lesser quality, can be stored separately then fermented to produce a second-grade wine. After pressing, a small quantity of sulphur is added to the must before racking.

RACKING

The juice produced by pressing still contains too many heavy, rough impurities (lees) to develop any elegant aromas during fermentation. The purification process is known as "racking" and it consists of depositing the solids in suspension onto the floor of the vat (sedimentation) by cooling the must down to 5° for 12 to 24 hours or more in certain difficult cases (chewy or damaged grapes). The clear juice has to be separated from the lees by racking. Then, using a racking hose and a candler, the vigneron checks the clarity of the liquid being pumped.

At this point, the must is finer and it has a more precise aroma. The problem, however, is to know when to stop racking. If done to excess, the must will become too bland and will lack the nutrients required for fermentation (mainly nitrogen-bearing elements). It is also possible to filter the lees and recover a second clear juice which, in certain cases, will produce a body and roundness not found in the first juice.

Filling a barrel with white wine in the Bordeaux area. CIVB.

ALCOHOLIC FERMENTATION

CONDITIONS

Fermentation can be done in barrels or vats. Barrels are used mainly for wines that are being kept for long-term aging while vats are used for wines with fast turnaround times, light lively whites drunk as an aperitif or with seafood. However, a number of excellent, well-known white wines have never seen a barrel so we should not be too quick to classify them. Sometimes, a vigneron will have to add yeasts selected in a laboratory to speed up the start of fermentation and avoid premature oxidation of the white must, which is particularly sensitive to this problem. Again, there are several schools of thought, especially in Burgundy where many people think that "indigenous" yeasts (specific to a cellar and specific grapes) are part of the definition of a *terroir*. The decision, which takes time and experience to acquire, is taken by each individual vigneron.

Ideally, fermentation should take place at a low temperature (18 to 22°C). This ensures continuity and, at the same time, prevents the destruction of certain aromas. The process should be relatively slow, lasting for eight to ten days. Turning sugar into alcohol should create as many aromas as possible.

In vats, the temperature should be regularly adjusted. It may be possible to aerate the must but this is not essential. In barrels, it is not so easy to adjust the temperature since it depends on the ambient temperature. The vigneron may add bentonite to the liquid to prevent the development of unpleasant odours.

END OF FERMENTATION

Fermentation stops of its own accord when the sugar level drops to less than 2 grams/litre. The winemaker can also stop fermentation when the sugar level has reached the level he wants, by lowering the temperature or adding sulphur. The aim is to leave some "residual" sugar to create semi-dry whites.

REMINDER: For dry whites, contrary to the process used for red wines and to guarantee a certain tartness and freshness, malolactic fermentation is generally not used. However, it is used in Burgundy where the basic acidity of the wine is too strong.

After testing the residual sugar level, the wine is racked to separate it from all the lees that build up during fermentation, mainly the residue from dead yeast. The wine is carefully protected from the air and loaded with carbon dioxide. It may be necessary to rack it several times to remove all the gas while limiting the effects of over-oxygenation. All that remains is to prepare for bottling, as described below, or to age the wine in a barrel to combine the aromas of vanilla, coconut and grilled meats with the scents of flowers, white fruits and citrus that are generally found in white wines.

A barrel could cause oxidation in white wines but, by using new or recent barrels (no more than two or three years old), the tannins released from the oak provide good protection.

A glass of dry white in the Bordeaux area. CIVB/ Yann Lacombe.

Sweet and medium wines

Specific characteristics

Sweet wines have a whole palette of very particular aromas and they are classified according to their sugar content. While medium-dry wines are similar to dry whites and contain only a few grams of sugar, medium wines can contain up to 45 grams and sweet wines even more.

Apart from this difference, which depends on the type of grape, the winemaking process differs in the sudden interruption of fermentation before the end of the process.

Choice of grapes

Before beginning to make the wine, the vigneron will have selected "golden grapes" in a process that usually involves two stages: raisining and noble rot.

Raisining means leaving the grapes to dry out on the stem in low atmospheric humidity, with plenty of air circulating around the fruit.

Noble rot is also a form of drying but it is due to damage from the "botritys cinerea" fungus so well-known to wine lovers, which damages the skins and leaves them fragile. This concentrates the sugar in the fruit and a chemical change affects the tissue of the skins as a result of enzymes carried by the fungus. This is why sweet and medium wines are so different to dry wines that are artificially sweetened.

Raisining. CIVB/V. Bengold.

Shortened fermentation

While fermentation is allowed to run its full course for dry whites, it is stopped prematurely for sweet and medium wines.

This interruption is essential because the must of sweet wines could reach 20 degrees of alcohol or more if it was completely fermented. It would then be impossible for the yeasts to survive in the excessively alcoholic environment and they would more or less asphyxiate themselves while turning the sugar into alcohol.

This sometimes occurs at about 15 or 16 degrees so fermentation has to be stopped before this temperature is reached. Several different methods can be used, depending on the equipment available:

The simplest method involves the sudden addition of a large dose of liquid sulphur to the wine, blocking the metabolism of the yeast and shutting down fermentation. Since the dose of sulphur is high, there is no need to add any more at a later stage. On the contrary, it may be necessary to air the wine to clear any unwanted odour.

A complementary method uses intense cold to block the metabolism of the yeast and cause the lees to sink very quickly. Since the lees contain some of the yeast, the risk of renewed fermentation is avoided by racking the wine as quickly as possible.

Free run wine. Photo by Patrick Izaute.

The final method that can be used is filtering the wine with a device based on tangential flow technology, which eliminates fine particles through small, porous, ceramic tubes. In this case, it is the combination of sulphur and the stripping of the lees that stabilises the wine with its residual sugar.

After this, the processes are the same as those used to produce dry white wine. However, medium and sweet wines are less sensitive to oxidation because of their "free" sulphur and their sugar content.

Rosés and clairet wines

Rosés occupy a middle ground between whites and reds. They are obtained from black grapes with colourless juice. Their popularity has risen steadily over the past decade, especially during the summer months. Their production is something of an art since it requires the vigneron to balance colour and tannins. There are three possible techniques: direct pressing, bleeding and the use of pink grapes.

THE TECHNIQUES

DIRECT PRESSING:

As soon as the grapes reach the cellar, they may be either crushed or placed directly in the press. They are then immediately pressed to release the colour as quickly as possible. The juice should remain in contact with the skins for as short a time as possible so that it does not become too red. The production process is the same as for white wines but, this time, the end product is pink in colour. This method is generally used in Provence, Burgundy, the Loire Valley and, in more recent years, in the Bordeaux area.

BLEEDING:

The vigneron begins production as if he were making a red wine: the grapes are placed in the vat. However, the remainder of the process is different. The grapes macerate for no more than 12 to 24 hours before the lightly-coloured juice is drawn off from the bottom of the vat, separating it from the skins and grape pips before they have time to produce too much colour. The juice is then placed in another vat for alcoholic fermentation.

In some regions, such as Provence, many vignerons use both methods, direct pressing and bleeding.

NOTE

Bleeding is also sometimes used to concentrate the colour of red wines. By removing lightly-coloured juice, the ratio of solids to liquid in the vat is increased. Washing this marc gives the wine colour and body. The more the wine remains in contact with the marc, the more it benefits from the potential tannins.

However, vignerons have to avoid excessive use of the bleeding technique because it can concentrate the defects and it does not necessarily

CIVS document.

produce a wine worthy of a *grand cru* from Médoc or Graves.

In short, direct pressing uses the entire grape in the production of a rosé while bleeding can be used to produce both rosés and reds, with what remains in the vat.

USE OF PINK GRAPES

In the Jura region, a specific pink grape variety is used, called "Poulsard". The production method is the same as the one used for red wines but with fairly long maceration. The juice extracted has an intense colour and a well-defined aroma.

RACKING

In every case, the wine has to be racked to remove any unpleasant "green" odours before fermentation. The vigneron may then add yeast. Alcoholic fermentation must start at a low temperature and it takes 10 to 14 days to complete. Malolactic fermentation, on the other hand, is not required because it would remove the acidity. By ignoring this step, the rosé retains a certain freshness.

It may be necessary to use finings to stabilise the wine and prevent unwanted deposits known in the trade as "protein breakdown".

SPECIAL CASE

In Champagne, it is permitted to blend red and white wines to produce a rosé. The wine is made using green Chardonnay grapes and black Pinot Meunier or Pinot Noir grapes. Since Pinots have very little natural colour, the juice produced by pressing them is only very slightly pink. This is also true of red Burgundy wines made with Pinot Noir grapes. Even after long maceration, they remain light red in colour, sometimes with hints of orange.

This explains why, by removing some of the colour, Pinot Noir grapes can be used to produce white champagne!

CELLARING

To ensure that a rosé retains its qualities, a vigneron will usually limit its exposure to oxygen and maintain the temperature of the vat at about 15°C.

Aging wine over fine lees also lengthens cellaring time.

However, it is difficult to keep rosés for long and, at the same time, maintain their primary qualities. They tend to lose their colour as they age, gradually taking on shades reminiscent of honey, quince jelly or plum. Direct pressed rosés in particular must be drunk while young to enjoy their freshness and fruitiness. Ideally, they should be drunk within two years of bottling, although the use of synthetic corks can increase this period slightly.

A glass of clairet wine.
Photo by Jacques Dubourg.

White and clairet wine in the Bordeaux area. CIVB.

CLAIRET

"Clairet" was the name given to red Bordeaux wine in the Middle Ages and English speakers still refer to wines from that area as "clarets". It is, then, a regional speciality with a colour similar to red wine but produced like a rosé with a slightly longer maceration stage (24 to 48 hours). Direct pressing is not used here, except with grapes that are overripe or damaged.

The characteristics of clairet are similar to rosé as regards aroma but its mouthfeel is more reminiscent of reds. It is also drunk chilled and it is sold mainly in the summer months because it is particularly good with barbecued meats.

Sparkling wines

CHARACTERSTICS OF SPARKLING WINES:

Until 1975, the term "sparkling" ("*crémant*" in French) was used for champagnes produced at half-pressure (3kg instead of 6kg). Now it is no longer used for champagnes. Instead, it refers to other sparkling wines. The term "*crémant*" has become an "AOC" (PDO, or protected designation of origin in English) in its own right and is used for:

Crémant de Bourgogne
Crémant de Loire
Crémant d'Alsace
Crémant de Bordeaux
Crémant de Limoux

PRODUCTION METHODS

These wines are made using the same method as champagne, with a great deal of work in the vat room and aging in the cellar.

WORK IN THE VAT ROOM

The grapes are hand picked fairly early in the season to ensure relatively high acidity. They are then pressed gently, producing approximately 100 litres of juice from 150 kilos of grapes. Indeed, Champagne's

Riddling racks. Louis de Grenelle cellars. Photo by Christophe Gagneur.

vignerons are generally recognised as the champions of the pressing process, a key stage in the production of a high-quality base wine ready to be turned into champagne. Juice is classified in three or four categories: first juice, which is often oxidised and discarded, the "*cuvée*" or main juices from the press and the "*tailles*" (one or two batches) produced after releasing some of the pressure, which are often of poorer quality. If the grapes are to be pressed several times, the marc has to be broken up by rotating the machine in the opposite direction. This causes harder extraction of the constituent parts of the grapes.

The must is then placed in a vat and kept at a temperature of between 20 and 22°C for two to three weeks until the first fermentation takes place naturally, using the yeasts contained in the grapes.

The dry wine is then bottled and the second fermentation will take place within the bottles, at a low temperature of about 10°C, to produce fine bubbles. The vigneron will already have added the "*liqueur de tirage*" consisting of sugar syrup and yeast. It is the yeasts that will cause the wine to ferment and produce carbon dioxide off gas (CO2). The wine assimilates the gas, giving it its bubbles. During this phase, the bottles are sealed with a temporary bung that will contain the yeasts and lees, and covered with a crown cap.

Vineyards in Alsace. Photo by Renault.

CELLARING

In the third stage of production, the bottles are taken to the cellar and set out on slats in cool, dark rooms where they are kept for a period of between nine months and five years depending on the vintage and the locality.

The next process is "riddling". The bottles are placed on racks, top downwards, and regularly turned, or "riddled", until the yeast deposits drop into the neck of the bottles. This is still sometimes done by hand, with the bottles given a quarter or one-eighth turn every day, but these days it is usually done using metal "gyropalettes" which rotate automatically.

Then comes disgorgement, when the neck of the bottles is plunged into a brine bath at a temperature of -25°C, producing a plug of ice. The sediment is then easily removed, thanks to the pressure from the carbon dioxide. The bung is removed for a moment then put back in place after topping up the level with the "*liqueur d'expédition*". The ingredients of this liquid are considered as a trade secret by winemakers but may include sugar, wine, *esprit de cognac* etc. It is these ingredients that give the end product its specific character as a *brut* or *demi-sec* champagne.

The bottle is then sealed with a cork forced into the neck of the bottle and held in place by a wire cage, or "*muselet*".

This is the production process for a sparkling wine defined by the aromatic notes that are specific to its *terroir* but, once disgorged, most bottles are put back in the cellar for a few months before being sold.

THE "RURAL METHOD"

In Southern France (famous for its Blanquette de Limoux and Clairette de Die), an age-old, "rural", method is used to produce sparkling wine. The bubbles are created by the natural sugar from non-fermented grapes. In this case, the first fermentation takes place directly in the bottle without losing any oxygen. Like the *liqueur de tirage* used in other sparkling wines, the gas produced using this method creates the bubbles. Most of these wines have an alcohol content of between 6° and 8°C and all of them contain residual sugar.

This method has the advantage of being natural. The drawback is the irregularity from one bottle to another.

A glass of sparkling wine in the Bordeaux area. CIVB/V. Bengold.

The final steps

After a few months (or a few years in some of the great vineyards) in a vat or in barrels, and before the heat of the summer has arrived, the wine is bottled. First, though, it must be tested by an oenologist, undergo preparation and be approved.

PREPARATION OF WINE

Before bottling, the wine must be stabilised so that it is crystal clear.

Firstly, the colouring agents in the wine may be stabilised. Too much colour can cause the precipitation of tartrates. Stabilisation can sometimes be achieved simply through the use of cold but, in most cases, it requires the addition of "finings", a traditional method that has been known since the days of the Ancient Romans. A small quantity of egg white, gelatine or casein is added to the wine where it forms flakes that suck up the colouring agents and tannins and attract any unwanted particles floating in the wine. These flakes are removed by racking.

Proteins in white wine have to be stabilised so that they do not produce a whitish sediment. This is done using a specific product called "bentonite".

FILTERING

Despite initial preparation, filtering is still necessary to ensure that the wines sold to consumers are clear and free of microbial growth. Any sediment and unwanted ferments are held back in the filters.

Several filtering techniques are available:

- layers of soil, often clay, of varying thickness
- cellulose plates. This is the commonest filtration method.
- manmade membranes or cartridges with different degrees of porosity.

APPROVAL

Until recently (July 2008), winemakers had to obtain AOC approval (protected designation of origin) for their wine every year before selling it. The approval procedure included tasting and chemical analysis. Now, checks are carried out at random and the wine is presumed to be up to standard if it complies with the specifications laid down for each *appellation*.

A committee of oenologists, merchants and vignerons carries out blind tasting on samples removed from vat rooms immediately before

Adding finings in the Bordeaux area. CIVB/CVM.

the wine is bottled. After this test, the experts decide whether or not the wine meets the quality standards required for that *appellation*. If it does not, further tests are conducted and penalties can be imposed by the *Institut National des Appellations d'Origine* (INAO). These can include an order preventing the winemaker from producing wine.

Bottles boxed up. Photo by Jacques Dubourg.

BOTTLING

There are various ways of bottling wine, depending on the equipment available:

The vigneron may have his or her own bottling plant but this is fairly unusual.

More commonly, vignerons use bottling trucks that can fill anything from 1,000 to 10,000 bottles an hour from vats. The truck is connected to the vats by a pipe through which the wine is pumped. The bottles are rinsed then filled, vacuum-corked and placed on a conveyor belt from which they are removed by workers.

Most vignerons attach great importance to the choice of cork, and most of them still use traditional natural cork. It is popular because it allows the wine to continue to breathe and develop in the bottle. The size of the cork can vary – it will be longer for wines that can be cellared for long period. Its quality is also important because, if it is not perfect or if there are a few cracks in the cork, the wine may leak out. These bottles are known in the trade as *"couleuses"*. There is also a risk of the wine being contaminated and acquiring a bad taste (the wine is described as being "corked") because of the quality of the cork or inadequate rinsing. This creates a highly damaging aromatic molecule called TCA (trichloroanisole) which very quickly gives the wine an unpleasant papier mâché taste. Such wines are usually sent back by consumers.

Some winegrowers are beginning to use screw tops or synthetic corks (especially for white wines and rosés), which are said to avoid giving the wine a corky taste. However, this is more of a cultural and technical decision and is not a cost-effective choice because, in many cases, these seals are more expensive than cork.

STORING WINE

Bottles are then placed in large wooden or metal crates, which are stacked up in the "bottle room" within the cellar.

The temperature and humidity in this area must be monitored to avoid rapid variations as they destabilise the wine. After a few years, such variations can also generate crystalline deposits in the form of tartrates. Excessive heat over a long period can cause the wines to develop and age prematurely. Light can degrade the colour and even taint the wine. This is why bottle rooms never have windows, or are located in basements.

Bottles in crates.
Photo by Jacques Dubourg.

LABELLING AND CAPSULING

Before the bottles can be sold, they have to be labelled and given their capsule. Both processes can be done at the end of the bottling line in the bottling truck. The bottles can then be placed in cardboard boxes.

Usually, though, these processes are carried out periodically at the vineyard, as and when the bottles are required to meet orders. The equipment used at vineyards is smaller.

Labelling and capsuling can be done in two separate machines but, to make the process easier, a winemaker will often use a single machine consisting of a labeller, an automatic

Manual wine capsuling machine.

capsule distributor and a foil crimping device.

The label is the wine's ID card. It carries a range of information, beginning with the category (table wine, local wine, higher quality wine of origin (AOVDQS) and protected designation of origin, PDO wines known in French as "AOC"). In the case of AOC wines, the information on the label can vary from one region to another. It includes the name of the vineyard, the *appellation*, the year, the volume, the alcohol content, the place of bottling and wording that has recently become mandatory i.e. "contains sulphites" and "not suitable for pregnant women". In the near future, bottles will also have to indicate, "contains egg" and "contains gelatine".

A wine buff generally checks the bottling method on the label and will usually only consider wines that are "estate bottled" ("*mis en bouteilles au domaine*", "*mis en bouteilles à la propriété*" or "*mis en bouteilles au château*"). This guarantees the authenticity of the wine because vignerons can only keep their own wines in their cellars and they can be inspected by the authorities. They cannot buy in another wine and store it on their premises, unlike merchants whose job it is to bottle wines from various *appellations* or even from vineyards all over the world. Merchants, of course, sell wines that are perfectly adequate. Indeed, they work hard to standardise quality from one year to the next by creating blends so that the wines they sell always have the same quality and have a recognisable taste.

Tasting a sparkling wine in the Bordeaux area. CIVB.

The capsule round the neck of the bottle improves its appearance and has replaced the wax used in days gone by. It protects the cork from a moth that can lay its eggs in the cork, causing massive damage. Within France, the capsule includes a small label indicating that the duties payable on the transport of wine have been paid to the Customs & Excise Department.

WINE BOXES, A SPECIAL CASE

When the winemaking process is finished, the wine can also be put into packaging known as BIB (Bag in Box), which is a registered trademark. This type of packaging is gaining in popularity at the present time.

The boxes contain a vacuum pouch containing 2 to 20 litres of wine, fitted with a tap. Their advantage is a long shelf life and the fact that the wine does not have to be drunk in a single sitting. Technical progress in corks and plastic film have increased shelf life to approximately eight months. Using the tap at the bottom of the bag, consumers can pour a glass of wine occasionally without the wine deteriorating inside the box.

Approval in the Bordeaux area.
CIVB/CVM.

Pouches are filled using a machine connected to the vat. Winemakers may have their own equipment or hire it. It creates a vacuum in the pouches to remove any risk of oxidation.

Wine box. Photo by Jacques Dubourg.

From cellar to glass

MARKETING

After completing all the stages in the winemaking process, the vigneron has to sell his wine and there are several marketing methods open to him.

The first method is cellar door sales and most vignerons are trying to develop this method because it is the most lucrative. They can also sell through wine shops, cafés, restaurants or supermarket chains. If they are members, they can also leave the

A traditional wine cellar at André Dussourt's vineyard in Scherwiller (Bas-Rhin).- 1790. Photo by Renault.

Oval wine cellar ("hélicave") by Harnois. Photo by Harnois.

marketing of the wine to a wine co-operative.

The second method involves selling to dealers or merchants.

A dealer is a person to whom a vigneron or cooperative sells the wine in the vat for wholesale distribution through the bulk wine market. A dealer sells on to a merchant.

If a merchant buys wine in bulk, he or she then bottles it and sells it through his or her own marketing network. A merchant can also buy wine in bottles directly from the vineyard and on-sell it.

STORING WINE AT HOME

As soon as you have bought your bottles of wine, they should be stored on their sides in a fairly cool cellar. The ideal temperature is between 12 and 15°C and any variations should be very gradual. The cellar must also be well aired but should not be draughty. Lighting should not be too bright. The cellar should not be too dry or too damp, with humidity levels of about 70%. Vibrations from the street are very damaging to wine. Wine is sensitive to smells so strong-smelling products such as fruit, vegetables or heating oil should not be stored in the same place.

If your cellar does not have all these features, you can try to improve it. Add ventilation if it is inadequate. Dry it out if it seems too damp by adding insulation panels which will stabilise the temperature.

If you do not have anywhere to store wine, you can buy a wine fridge, which maintains the temperature and humidity at appropriate levels.

This completes the various steps taken by vignerons to produce wine. For your part, you have put the wine in your cellar and ensured that the conditions are right. Now you can open a bottle, pour the wine into a glass, breathe it in, admire its robe and, at last, appreciate its flavour.

Barrels on the banks of the River Weiss. Photo by Renault.

The vineyards in Hunawihr (Haut-Rhin). Photo by Renault.

Glossary

Acabailles: celebrations and a meal held at the end of the grape harvest.

Acidity: the presence of acid substances that are essential for wine which is to be cellared.

Alcoholic fermentation: a microbiological stage during which yeasts develop away from the air and turn the grape sugar into alcohol and carbon dioxide.

Approval (*agrément*): testing of the wine by a committee, which grants the vigneron the right to use the term *"appellation d'origine contrôlée"* (protected designation of origin: AOC in French, PDO in English).

Anthocyanins: ingredients that give the wine its colour.

AOC: an abbreviation indicating a protected designation of origin (PDO in English).

Bordeaux (Gironde), a world-famous PDO. Photo by Gisserot.

Grape pickers in Ribeauvillé (Haut-Rhin). Photo by Renault.

Aroma: the main fragrance exhaled by the wine (fruit, fragrance, bouquet).

Bidule: a small temporary plug made of plastic which collects the yeast from sparkling wine.

Bleeding (*saignée*): a technique that requires a quantity of juice (up to 25%) to be removed in order to create a better quality red wine.

Blending: mixing wines from different grape varieties to produce a wine that is balanced and of constant quality.

Botrytis: noble rot.

Bouquet: all the olfactory feelings created by the wine.

Crushing: a process designed to crush the grapes.

Delestage: the reinjection of the must drawn off from the vat back over the cap to facilitate the extraction of tannins (also known as "rack and return").

Devatting: transferring the wine from the vat in which it has fermented into barrels.

Drawing off: transferring the wine from one vat or barrel to another to remove the lees.

Epinette: small secateurs used by grape pickers.

Fatty: an adjective describing a smooth wine.

Fining: a clarification technique which consists of adding a product to the barrels to coagulate and precipitate the particles in suspension in the wine.

Firkin: a large wooden barrel containing 50 to 300 hectolitres.

Free sulphur: the portion of sulphur that has not combined with the components of the wine.

Gerbaude: a term used in certain regions of France to describe the celebrations and meal that mark the end of the grape harvest.

Lees: the residue or deposit remaining in the bottom of wine containers after fermentation or during storage.

Maceration: contact between the grape skins and pips and the juice to give red wine its colour and tannins.

Malolactic fermentation: the second fermentation during which bacteria turn the malic acid from the grapes into lactic acid and carbon dioxide.

Marc: residue from the pressing of fresh grapes, whether or not they have fermented (also known as "pomace").

Must: must is unfermented grape juice obtained by pressing or crushing, used to produce wine by a process of alcoholic fermentation.

Organoleptic: an adjective referring to the characteristics that our various senses perceive during tasting.

Pressing: a process whereby grape marc is pressed to extract the juice.

Pumping over: a process carried out after the first fermentation. The grape juice is drawn off from the bottom of the vat and pumped back in at the top.

Pumping over red wine in the Bordeaux area. CIVB/Ph. Roy.

Punching down: the pushing of a long pole, or paddle, through the marc to facilitate the extraction of tannins.

Racking: the removal of certain particles contained in the must after mechanical processes.

Raisining: a late harvesting technique that involves leaving the grapes to dry out on the vine.

Running off: the process conducted after fermentation to separate the liquid (called the "run wine") from the solids (the "marc").

Stems: all the pedicels in a bunch of grapes.

Stripping or destemming: this operation consists of removing the grapes from the stem.

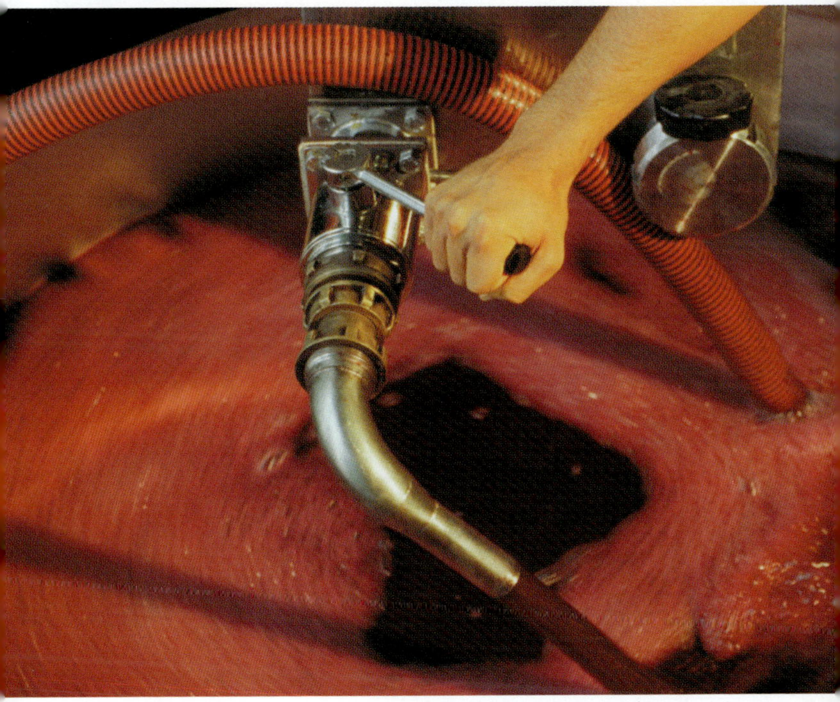

GIPCRCRV document.

Sulphiting: the addition of sulphite to must to protect it against disease.

Supple: an adjective describing a wine that is lush to the nose and produces a feeling on the palate similar to the feeling produced by handling a soft fabric.

Tangential: an adjective referring to a specific filtering technique used to remove fine, unwanted particles from the wine.

Tannins: organic products from the stems, skin and pips of grapes allowing the wine to age.

Topping up: a process by which the level of liquid in barrels is brought back to its maximum during cellaring.

Winemaking: all the stages between fermentation and bottling. The term can also be extended to include the aging of bottles in the cellar.

Yeast: microscopic fungi that cause fermentation and turn grape juice into wine.

Vines in Alsace. Photo by Renault.

Contents

Imprimé et façonné par Pollina Luçon 85 n° d'impression : L75100
Imprimé en France
PEFC 10-31-2065